New Tracks, **Night Falling**

Jeanne Murray Walker

New Tracks, **Night Falling**

William B. Eerdmans Publishing Company

Grand Rapids, Michigan / Cambridge, U.K.

Published 2009 by
Wm. B. Eerdmans Publishing Co.
2140 Oak Industrial Drive N.E., Grand Rapids, Michigan 49505 /
P.O. Box 163, Cambridge CB3 9PU U.K.

Printed in the United States of America

15 14 13 12 11 10 09   7 6 5 4 3 2 1

Library of Congress Cataloging-in-Publication Data

Walker, Jeanne Murray.
    New tracks, night falling / Jeanne Murray Walker.
        p.   cm.
    ISBN 978-0-8028-2572-8 (pbk. : alk. paper)
    I. Title.
    PS3573.A425336N49   2009
    811'.54 — dc22

                                        2008048955

www.eerdmans.com

For Molly, Jack, Matt, and Bobbie

Contents

Choices

Tracks

Resolutions

Preface

Poetry has given people solace for thousands of years, entertained and nurtured them, but these days it seems odd to many of us. It smacks of elitism. To read it seems rather like reading a foreign language. Furthermore, it doesn't affect the stock market, and it can't change the course of a war. Why read poetry?

For me, reading a poem is like following tracks to an interior realm. Say it's been snowing all day, and you have cabin fever and decide to go to the park. On the broad expanse of a snowy field spreading before you, you spot paw prints leading to a dense stand of maples. You don't know what kind of animal it is or even how big, but suddenly you realize you're not the only one here. You imagine eyes shining at you from the trees. Maybe you decide to follow the tracks.

Almost certainly you've felt particularly alive in this way, oddly jolted, visited for a moment by a sense of mystery. It's like a nudge that seems to come out of nowhere. Not a hammer blow — more like a hunch or a premonition with a jacket of words around it. It gives language to experience, the feelings of love and despair, of joy and resentment that define our interior lives every day. It acknowledges the strangeness of being human.

Poems are not, as many people fear, hieroglyphics that are hopelessly indecipherable by all but a few readers. And they're not some elaborate system of double-talk which has been designed to hide meaning. Poems use the very same strategies we all use when we talk to one another: the sturdy, reliable vocabulary of English, figures of speech, metaphor, repeated sounds, rhythm. Of course, poems are more condensed than the language we use at the supermarket. Poets tend not to explain much. But if you pay attention, in a good poem you will hear a human voice talking to you.

In fact, it's possible that poems are the most natural kind of human talk. Little kids sound like poets until we teach them to stop using startling metaphors and start using abstractions. Occasionally at the beginning of the semester, one of my students tells me that she's all about math, she's got no sense of poetry whatsoever. But I make every student write a sonnet, and a surprising number of the good sonnets are written by students who consider themselves poetically disabled. I know a good sonnet when I see one, in part, because even though the form is prefabricated, it reads like the record of one person's unpredictable journey toward mystery.

The mystery that ignites the best poems, the mystery to which those poems direct their readers, is the same mystery that lies at the heart of all we know and want. Though there's plenty we don't know about how nature operates, what obsesses most of us is not the mystery of how things function. Oh sure, I'm fascinated with the human genome project, and I salute the discovery of ice on Mars as a triumph. But what really baffles me is why I am so prone to do exactly what I don't want to do. And I don't understand why we humans keep opting for war. Other mysteries drive me crazy too. Why do we have to die, and to what unfathomable place does death bring us? How is it possible to overcome the deep loneliness of being a separate, conscious human being? Why does grace sometimes visit us out of the blue? These are the questions that finally drive me to God.

I don't know when it started — maybe sometime after the catastrophic, gorgeous Tuesday morning, 9/11. I have begun to worry about how driven by fear we are in this country, and how divided. As our children are shipped back from Iraq in boxes, the conflict alienates us from one another. We are scared of those who don't fit in.

There's talk about a flu pandemic and infections against which we have no antibiotics. We are becoming aware of how, by abusing nature, we are permanently changing the earth and its weather. It feels like night is falling.

It's August as I write this. No rain for weeks. I'm out watering our impatiens, clatching with my favorite neighbor across our common hedge. I mention the upcoming election. She ducks, suddenly needing to water her rare perennials, and I think I understand. She doesn't want to offend me by taking the wrong side. This polite evasion reminds me how on my 45-mile drive home, one SUV driver did not try to avoid connection, but sought it, aiming his gleaming black, satanic vehicle at me. I swerved to prevent a collision, but the near-miss has left me with a headache.

I go into our house and struggle to open a new bottle of aspirin. I pry at the cap, with no luck. Then I find a scissors. When that doesn't work, I grab a can opener from the kitchen drawer. Finally, I gnaw at the bottle with my teeth, cursing whatever pharmaceutical terrorists make this kind of armor necessary. Later I switch on the TV and watch a close-up of a fat, gorgeous double cheeseburger guided by the hands of a teenager toward his mouth. Six more commercials follow. I switch the TV off, fed up with spin.

About five years ago, the spookiness of all this alienation began to wake me up at night. I felt mute because I believed that a poet has no business writing about politics and war. Homer did. Milton did. But no one reads epics anymore. The personal lyric that poets since Wordsworth bequeathed to us tends to collapse under the weight of political and social issues. How can I write about what divides us? These are gigantic matters of the soul.

Night is falling, I think. I know that's a little hysterical, but that's what I think. Night is falling.

Then I feel a nudge, an idea, a small shock of insight. I get up from the couch in front of our TV, slip down the stairs to the kitchen, take out five fat red tomatoes, and begin to chop them. I chop with excessive force. I chop for dear life. A poem takes shape in my head, a poem of complaint.

The ability to articulate a problem is the beginning of healing. Even complaint is a sign of hope. Writing poetry, at least for me, has never been a way of explaining the nature of things. Most often it is a wistful groping toward truth. It is as unpredictable as following tracks in the snow. It is a learning process through which I have discovered most of what I know. If I roll up my sleeves and work wholeheartedly at meter and metaphor, which is my job as a poet, some kind of quiet truth occasionally shows up. I suspect this is typical of what happens to most writers and painters and musicians. In our work lies the secret of our healing.

A poet organizes the hunt so others can join in, pushing as far as possible toward what is, perhaps, finally unknowable. The truth may be too dazzling for us to see clearly, but I do not believe it is random or meaningless. Einstein said, "God does not play dice with the universe." He is reliable. I have faith that the tracks we see lead to understanding of our human dilemmas and sometimes take us to places that are holy.

I invite you to join me in this process, to read these poems and follow the clues with me. This book starts with separations brought by war and illness and death. In a small house in Pipestone, Minnesota, one day after 9/11, my venerable bachelor uncle died while watching on his ancient black-and-white TV — repeatedly, as we all did — the planes strike the Towers. He was alone. His heart couldn't take it. From that and other kinds of separation, the book goes on to examine specific moments of personal choice and how those choices change history. Then it turns to pursue signs and inklings: sparrows, those tracks in the snow, shadows, the sound of a bell, headlights, a leaf. These lead to resolutions. The poems in the last section are conclusions, I suppose, but like New Year's resolutions, they also mark beginnings.

———————

I sweep the cold, juicy red bits of tomato from the cutting board into the palm of my hand and toss them into a pan of hot olive oil. The dear familiar physicality of tomatoes and fire and a knife and the cutting board is almost enough to make me feel better. Outside in the garden, tomatoes swell and redden. I hope they don't wither in the drought. The bits of tomato in the pan sizzle and spit as if they're alive. Then, suddenly, it seems possible to imagine rain. I can hear it moving toward us across the field. And it pours.

JEANNE MURRAY WALKER
Merion Station, PA

Separations

Neighbor

You've gone AWOL and only Jesus
can bring you back. Not tears,
not rain. Not this poem.
You are an ocean who's abandoned
its bed. The sky who folded up
its blue tent and traveled south.

What remained of you, they sent
to fire. Before we sat in the meetinghouse
to make your legend, I could almost feel
your spirit, the daredevil
cartoon superwoman, peel itself
from the wall of death
and shove off to investigate.
So tell me what you learned.
Is it possible to breathe
astral, heavenly air? And tell me,

was it worth it? — all that Sturm und Drang
we pitched against death,
who'd rather work in secret —
roads under construction at night,
collusion over charts, rampage of doctors —
to prevent as long as possible
the clever kleptomaniac from winning.
He could only steal your body.
Which I miss, it's true, oh god,
it's true. The screen door you
banged every afternoon, now silent.

Elegy: Lloyd Aderhold, d. September 12, 2001

Snow drifted over him as he dozed in the cold breezeway
in his Naugahyde recliner. From here
he looked like a character sealed in a snow globe
representing one way a man could freeze to death.
On days I phoned him, I imagined him
brushing snow off, rising like a great walrus
to shuffle inside the kitchen and pick up.
Crops and weather is what we talked, crops

and weather. Not that I called for love,
exactly, but so that if he died, he wouldn't remain
inside the house for months. He was
detailed, grave, and civil. When we flew
to bury him, we found three suits laid out across his bed,
for our convenience, to choose his shroud,
and on the table, scraps of paper webbed in spidery printing,
the exact words he'd said to me for years

with dates of our calls. But my tall bachelor uncle,
what you didn't write down, what you had no words for,
was the way your heart broke finally,
all day watching airplanes inside your TV
penetrate the Towers. How you took
that fire into your lonely body, how
you took the blows like javelins to your chest.

Revenge

Call it tulips, the red and orange petals
that bloomed from the stalks of the Trade Towers,
flowers you held out in the Spanish-blue vase of sky,
performance art of such originality
we're spellbound.
                    This tragedy has cousins:
the tornado with lathe and plaster sailing
through the air. The flood three years ago:
our houses bobbing gleefully toward the ocean.

But you nurtured your grudge, like the boy
who practices beside his open window
in the heat, listening to the lucky neighbor children
off to the beach, their language loose
with a belief in joy that pierces his heart.

Think of him sliding into the cool cave
of Rachmaninoff, feeling his way towards
his black-heart grudge. He dwells there
in the wet dark, perfecting notes that glitter
like knives until his grievance grows so clear,
the kids seem less important than the buttons
on his shirt. *See if I care* is what he means.
Or rather, *Someday I will show you
I am not what you think.*

I wonder if that's how it was
as police glean maps, false papers, pilots'
licenses from your secret rooms. All
those years of practicing before the day
you soloed, before you made your
gift and your intention public.

Take Heart

Who can grieve for it all?
The standard-bearer, seeing
his right hand shot off, grabs the flag
with his left and shouts *God bless America!*
as he charges up the hill. An Iraqi child
shoos flies from her brother's corpse.
News, they call it.
The gospel of atrocities.

Seeing a lemon, incandescent with light,
hearing the cry of a bird with the sky
caught in its throat, I almost forget.
I woo heartlessness.
Would it necessarily
make me cruel or stupid?

On one of those cooking shows,
a new chef appears. *Take heart,*
for instance, he says, paging
through his cookbook: Heart.

A delicious muscle grilled,
baked, or steamed with bamboo shoots.
Like liver or kidneys, but harder to find
in the better markets. Looking for a heart,
he opens his map of our neighborhood.
He pulls on his coat and hat.
The bags under his eyes are the color of nickels.

We Have Nothing to Fear but Fear Itself

There were days heaven seemed easy.
Days it came right down,
drifting into my hair like pollen.
Then it seemed natural to pray.
Then everyone showed up in my prayer.
Talking was prayer, unlocking
the door was. In those days,
I was all praise and thank you's,
without even moving my lips.

People will die for less —
to be taken into the sky like that,
to walk as the holy do, without
exegesis, without needing
to explain.
                    Now
the clouds above Chestnut Street
have clicked shut, locking us out.
One day we have a hunch. Next day
a grudge divides us.

Oh, to live before we made
separations our thesis. As if
a child had drawn a line with a crayon:
here's the sky, here's the earth,
here's a woman, here's everything else.
Its name is Enemy.

After 9/11: The Separations

It's summer, the young stepping
    confident as barons between horn blasts
        on Lex Avenue, my hand brushing

the arm of someone — who? — lonely, desperate,
    planning, maybe, to take a building down.
        And I think of those in hospitals,

sitting in booths, recording histories quietly,
    separating the crazy from the sane.
        How like us they are, but how different

in their power. And policemen, for example.
    Though I know they could be split
        like watermelons, sometimes

I envision them as gods. Like a child,
    sometimes I'd like to beg them, *Take me home.*
        And yet, I curse such separations.

Last June I took my son
    for his driver's license. He had failed once.
        It was the luck of the draw, which examiner,

and my son was eighteen, desperate
    to be a man. The codger
        with the white hair, awesome in his power,

slid in beside my son. It was then, before
    he gave us the license, I wanted to ask him,
        Are you afraid of us?

I wanted to warn him, *Don't get into
    just any car that drives up.*
        But I didn't.

He might have thought it was a trick.
  We could have been just anybody.
    To him we must have looked like the public.

Anger

For years I've knelt to button the coats of children.
I've walked on my knees for years.
When is sweetness that puts up with anything
really the softness that precedes rot?
I want my anger back.

Outside, rain thrashes like Jesus
whipping the money-changers from the temple.
I watch an oak thrust its roots into the sky.

Under the Schuylkill's pendulous floodwater
the riverbed shifts its shape
until its stones finally assent
to whatever the furious water wants.

Some things call for anger.
The mayor's limo, windows darkened
to keep the luxury in, slides
through streets of houses, broken
like the broken teeth of old men.
The bribes are tall and good-looking.
Money clutches votes in its beautiful hands.

Let the wind come. Let it
rip off shutters and turn them
into axes. Let mahogany credenzas float
down Main Street like the prows
of ships. Let brokers tie themselves
to chairs for safety. Let the naked
mayor float by on a mattress.

A Sign

This painting is from my early work, he told me —
the stubble-faced art professor from Westchester State
whose wallet had been stolen, car broken down
on the way to his gallery. He needed twelve bucks

to get there. Oh, I've been taken. Plenty. It's not
the money, it's the song you can't get out of your head:
Gullible, gullible. He waited as I thought it over.
He stood aloof and lordly.

This happened before cell phones,
you understand, and he had perfect pitch,
like our piano tuner, knowing the words
to play me. What I decided

would shape my future. I felt that.
In my personal museum of the gruesome:
I had refused a father milk for his baby, refused
the babushka-mouth-harp woman a single quarter.

When is it too late to go back?
Can the heart close up shop forever?
All right, I thought, *if a red Chevrolet goes by,*
I'll take it as a sign. A sign of what?

I wanted a signal clear as a phone call.
Articulate as the boy I loved at fifteen, who one day
stole up behind me, pressed the hands I dreamed of
over my eyes, and whispered, "Guess who?"

Tangent

I am on the wrong road, where a sudden
homeboy is smacking a ball of string
with a chair rung, running to first base —

someone's jalopy on cement blocks. So now I know
how familiar a tangent can look until
it vaults up in the dark to rip your heart out.

I steer a path around double-parked cars,
my hand gripping my Toyota's throbbing shift,
quoting "The Road Less Traveled,"

swerving to miss Slim Hips just before
he removes me from the face of the earth
with his mouth. This must be a dream. Another me

is driving the expressway home to wine and baked salmon,
already drunk on Frost, kissing my husband
hello, sorting through the usual bills.

And now the kid with the mouth casts me
the glance of a furious lover about to make things clear.
I want to lean out and plead with him to woo

the alphabet with that sexy mouth,
to learn to read, Man, read, Man, read,
but somewhere far away I am gliding

through my house by rote, shedding my coat.
Maybe tomorrow I will turn up missing,
I'll be the blur at that dark window,

the dark mother who's lost her son, watching for him
while someone else floats down the street
in the stiff silver crinolines of a new Toyota,

learning that her main road has been
a tangent, wondering how long it takes
to know which is which.

Ritual

As the alarm shrilled through the twelve-seater
   and the pilot scrambled for his manual,
      I wanted someone to stand up
and lead us in song,
   or possibly prayer

but we sat beneath our personal
   air nozzles, unable to shake
      our useful habit of reserve.
Beside me a man read *Time*.
   A girl pulled out her barf bag

and I thought of sending my voice out
   like a skater on a pond to say something
      true and beautiful and daring,
how not a sparrow, maybe,
   falls without notice,

but our plane was yo-yoing
   like a heart machine gone bonkers,
      graphing the steep W's
of our collective fall,
   and my voice burrowed

for safety in my chest,
   and I turned, we all turned
      to our captain, a simple boy in earphones
fighting to steer the little duck
   paddling for its life

in a dark, anonymous sky,
   and I thought how odd it was
      that our names would appear
together in the papers,
   like the cast of a musical,

who died, separately, without ritual or touching.

Domestic Violence

The sky was swimming-pool blue and I could almost
   imagine angels, the old ones with blond curls,
      gazing down at us, the enigmas

they've agreed to guard, while through the open window
   in a brownstone behind me
      a voice climbed up a ladder of threats,

then another drew a dark warning line in air.
   Not so different from our own quarrels,
      but headed, I could hear, for death,

and I wanted nothing more than to escape.
   But tact or decency, or some policeman inside me,
      kept me rooted to the sidewalk. *Do unto others*

as I would have done to me. But what do I want?
   Oh, maybe some of what we want is simple.
      Grass wants to grow in the sidewalk cracks.

The sparrow wants to burst free of the barn
   before the fire kills her. But what about
      the parents who moved to Lockerbie

so that every morning they could see where
   their daughter fell, burning, from the Pan Am jet?
      Who can predict? Our complex desires,

our self-deceptions! Behind me the voices,
   wild now as bulls broken out of their pens,
      charging one another. And above, the old angels

avert their eyes again. It's I who must decide:
   The savagery of the human heart and the secrecy it longs for,
      or the law it knows it needs?

History

starts as an ache in the throat.
Take Moses, for instance, walking through the Red Sea
in front of gap-toothed, limping slaves

he's learning are not stupid. The conviction
gathers in him: they need laws. To get laws
he would have to walk into the mouth of God.

And maybe he will. After all, one oddity has led
to another. The locust plague accomplished
everything he could imagine.

When he tossed his rod down, it turned into a snake,
and now the Promised Land is raising
her forehead to smile at them. Still,

history slows him down like a broken bone in his ankle.
Everyone he loves, he left in Egypt!
After the tenth plague, he can't stop imagining

his favorite uncle laid out in the stone sarcophagus.
What else, he wonders, could he have done
when God told him to throw down the rod

against his family, the God who last night
killed every firstborn in Egypt. By *firstborn*
did God mean his mother's oldest brother,

the Prince, who, like a faithful camel,
carried him all over the palace on his back?

To Mr. Auden in a Time of War

In the nightmare of the dark
All the dogs of Europe bark,
And the living nations wait,
Each sequestered in its hate.

W. H. Auden

In this dark time I want to make light bigger,
to toss it in the air like a pizza chef,
to stick my fists in, stretching it
till I can get both arms into radiance up to the elbow
and spin it above us.

But oh, dark is such a genius at argument,
using all the rhetorical figures.
And you aren't bad yourself, Mr. Auden,
elucidating war, explaining how each nation
becomes a blind man,
alone in his own dark, gripping
his cane, unable to cross the street to his lover
who, let's say, waits by the pizza parlor —
lost, unable even to see her,
unable to sing out, the way a lover
should, *Susan, it's you!*

In truth, the dark is personal, fluttering
like a red moth behind my eyelids.
My Texas cousin lies dead this afternoon,
and his widow's at the funeral home
with their child, trying to explain where he has gone.
Isn't that the brilliant final move of dark —
Poof! — to separate us from each other?

Between us, Mr. Auden, we have made darkness
so dark there's no escape,

except I wonder, isn't seeing darkness
seeing? Maybe that's why,
as Susan crosses, right,
to find her lover, as she takes his hand,
I see a stain just above the horizon.
The sky, leaking sweet violet light.

Gesture Upwards

I have promised to pray for a friend,
the way one promises when there are no solutions.
Here in Vermont the cold is slowing things down —
the way a squad car parked along the shoulder
slows traffic. The birches are migrating
to precincts of yellow. From there
they'll take their permanent leave.
I pull into a lane to study how they do it.
Beside the road a cat stretches, pouring herself
towards her paws. Birds scatter, fanning out
as if flung into the sky, as if someone
wants to demonstrate the physics of motion,
nothing about bones and muscles, just a flawless
gesture upwards. The leaves float down so slowly
it feels as if my car is sinking under water.
I am a fish, watching the sea turn
gold. Like the sole of a foot, a yellow leaf
steps on the windshield, then another,
and another — feet, walking on water.

Choices

Bergman

I am at the movies, practicing the discipline
of the sane, taking the characters
to my heart, while reminding myself
they're not me. Red scarf flying against snow
like a flag of happiness. Their looks meeting
across a table in the café. That blessing of first love,
to have your gaze returned. Then later,
the misunderstanding, that bewildering
shift. His face looming big as a baseball field,
his eyebrows flying like hysterical seagulls.
He has just begun to shout when the film gets stuck,

the same ugly word, ugly word he can't call back,
a word she can't forgive. In the booth
a kid bends over the projector,
a god now, performing small maneuvers of love
as we stare at the palpitating hoo-ha
of the man's mouth, the cruelty in her eyes,

watching how habit can harden the heart, how
it's possible to cross into a country beyond choice,
beyond remorse, beyond forgiveness,
how even Pharaoh didn't know exactly when,
between the first and tenth plagues,
he found himself inside the answer he could never
change, the way we are stuck in the film's repeating

stutter. Until the boy cuts it. We go home early.
I turn the key in the lock, hearing the wind in the trees,
the sound of God weeping, his heart shattered on
the stubborn mystery of the human will.

Adam's Choice

It must have been a windy night like this,
    the trees swaying and hissing,
        tossing their hair in desperate gestures,
when he broke out of the spell
    and realized it wasn't fair.
        He never chose her.

When he woke up, she stood before him
    like a bright goblet filling up with water.
        He was thirsty. *How splendid*

it can be to drink when you're thirsty,
    was what he thought. He was that young.
    Now he realizes there is a stain

spreading on his heart, that the name
    she gave the yak chafes him,
        and she sings off-key. He never chose

her. He'd like to grab his knife
    and cut off her song,
        but rain is slanting down

and she is running toward him, her eyes terrified
    under the bending, cracking maples,
        and a curtain pulls back in him

and he takes her into his arms
    and begins the long journey toward
        learning to love what he's been given.

So She Became an Ancestor of Jesus

And the spy . . . came into a harlot's house,
named Rahab, and lodged there.

Joshua 2:1

In the pomegranate market
he's surely heard my name, Rahab,
tall woman who loves too easily.
Woman with ravens flying in her eyes,
a cord marking her business,
red as bloody sunset. And he's
seen me walking, I'd guess, with the white jar
balanced on my head. *Ship's Sail,*
they call me. From this window
I see him riding shadows,
biding his time, spying out our
town for Jehovah. He doesn't care
for us. All he wants
is to let himself down on the other side
of the city wall, to swing to safety
in the mountains. And I should help him?

Then why does his pulse beat in my neck
as our police track him down every
street and opening? So near
now I can hear him breathing. Running
makes him forget exactly who he is,
a good man, a family man. To be seen in
the red-light district hurts him like a stitch
in his side. They're closing in, now.
It's ring my bell or die.

When I open, he fingers his collar
nervously. I can feel blue-black feathers
whir up in my eyes. I touch his shoulder
and whisper, *Come in. Come in.*

Laying Down the Stone

"Take you . . . out of every tribe a man . . ."

Joshua 4:1-9

He thinks of himself as thin,
his arms scrawny, himself
famous for being slightly gullible,

so how improbable
that out of the thousand men in his tribe,
Joshua would bellow his name.

Carry the stone to Gilgal
where it will stand forever
for the tribe of Levi. When he lifts it,

it shifts like a planet, grinding
across his forearm, leaving
striations of bright blood. He

staggers. Who is he now,
but the man who carries a stone?
Then suddenly a fist of weightlessness

in the stone's heart opens
its fingers and spreads towards
the baggy granite skin. His own bones

float like notes from flutes,
and he wonders at how nothing is itself,
at how yesterday the River Jordan stopped

and stood in a heap before the holy ark,
at how water and stone and flesh obeyed
like trained camels. And now, as he thrusts it

into its nook beside eleven others,
he can almost feel the hands of his children's
children's children rest on his back.

Not yet born, and yet he watches them
approach shyly, touch it, then walk off,
A tribe of them bending and swaying

like fig trees, delicate and free on the horizon.

Silent Night

— For Marjorie Maddox

The holly bush stands by the peeling door
she stumbled through last night, under the stare
of curious eyes. She didn't make it far

beyond the first stall, so she lay down there
to let her body have its way with her.
Rubbing her back, he braced himself against the door.

Maybe she wished that she could give it up —
the greeting of the angel on her stoop,
her *yes,* the thousand future paintings. She would swap

it all to stop this lava. Not to erupt
with God. To halt the bleeding of the Infinite
into that barn. Peaceful? Silent? It was abrupt,

loud, violent. She was blown apart. Body went
one way, she went another. Just to keep her blunt
place in the world, she sent her eyes hunting

the holly: that woman, sister, aunt, waiting
patiently outside to help. As God came ripping
through — a wild train — her eyes kept holding

that tree. She rests now. Wind is leaking
into the barn; the animals are sleeping.
Outside, the holy holly bough is breaking.

Rich Young Ruler

*And Jesus . . . said, "How hardly shall they that have riches
enter into the Kingdom of Heaven."*

Mark 10:23

Maybe he's traveled. Maybe his heart is a runaway stallion,
greedy for each strange country till he gets there,
when he blows its newness away like milkweed silk.
Because there are no countries left, the known world
being not that big, as Alexander wept
to discover, and now that he stands at the edge,
he sees that the edge is in him, a police limit
he learned long before he knew what he was learning,
which he can never, therefore, exceed.
Because he's reached the final country.
But he feels empty, vacant, frightened, light-headed
with need for another.

And because he swears
that if he ever finds another, he will be grateful, he will
explore meticulously every alley, archway,
gutter, and pore, spacing between sips, savoring
the taste. Still, when a crack appears, improbably,
in the carpenter's sentence, when a door swings
open, when he finds himself straddling
mountain passes, gazing down at green trees,
curlicue vines, water leaping,
the place hibiscus-mad, fruitful, still and eternal,
he whispers, *No thanks, unfortunately, no.*

The Choice

She stands high above the river,
watching her wild friends
dive like naked questions,
making holes in the sky.
She is an outsider on the reeling morning,
a dust fleck on the lens of a projector
that clings to the side of the movie's action.

Below her, one by one, her friends shoot up
from the dark center of the water
and bob now, white as teeth,
downstream away from her.
Each feels like a raw electric nerve marking
a place she didn't have the guts to jump.

She begins to feel, far down in her brain,
today is the exact day she will die.
That fact feels hard and gorgeous as a pearl.

Who will tell her it's not gorgeous enough?
Who will say she should not go?
Not today. Not yet. Who will explain all that she still might love?
No one watches while she pulls off her jeans,
finds her tall white body
and sends it,
heart exploding, brain
exploding, toward the black waterfall.

Just As I Am

The organ swings into the invitation hymn,
slinging us around the known world
toward the apogee of surrender,
O Muse of Scripture, Muse of Choice,
Muse of the Sawdust Trail.
I look at my hand resting on this oak pew,
shaped like Asia, a million cells teeming,
blood pumping, going on with its normal
irreligious, hungry life.
Things are being decided. We are
singing "Just As I Am, without One Plea,"
the fourth verse, over. My right hand
is aware of the soprano next to me,
balancing on her catwalk of steep chords.
It longs to fly up to that soaring obligato.
Just raise your hand, the Evangelist pleads,
if you want God to use you.
My right hand twitches, fighting against
the skyward tug of the kite string.
What my hand has been taught —
marks on paper, numbers, letters,
postulates — breaks down.
The whole repertoire of my life
is practice for this moment.
I try to make myself restful, empty, nothing
but an interval
before the generous right hand,
and the sinister left, decide.

The Failing Student

In the old stories it's always worth the trouble,
    but this time you doubt it.
For months she's hidden herself
    at the brambled rim of that steep hill,

bleating for help as the wind
    sings its increasingly wicked song.
Winter is coming. It means business.
    You think of yourself as the field

she's absent from, as the shepherd who must
    find her. You begin to understand
how mercy can start as little more
    than a direction you can move in,

how your heart hates death.
    You begin picking your way toward her
through a whole vocabulary
    of wildflowers and thorns.

The Road South

How the mind labors to make some use of suffering,
to ease the heart's burden. Watch the twenty-year-old tanner
bend in his backyard, the stink of lye rising
while he scribbles couplets to sell for twopence with the gloves,

the need for pounds pounding down bright concourses
of his blood. His wife and three children squabbling
inside. Oh, it's the old story. Desire pitched
against rampant minuses, red ink exploding

on the ledger, the need to make something
out of nothing wherever he looked: cracking his egg
at breakfast, the shell seemed like a purse
to keep the white and yolk in. As his desperation

grows heavy, it splits into names, each name
him, each gnawed by the lion's tooth of love and loathing,
a mob bursting the walls of his young heart.
Reading the map of Stratford in grammar school,

did he search for a road to some place
where he could become Shakespeare?
When did the word *London* open its door?
When did he see the O as possibility — crown, globe,

thatched octagon, a stage with voices raging
in a tongue that even he could barely guess?
When did he guess that if God loves us, it must be
because he knows our aptitude for suffering?

Let's say one afternoon a shadow by the name of Bottom
saw him staring down the road and drew
the map to London on a pebble. Let's say the tanner,
looking innocent, slipped it in his pocket.

Gloves

I'd studied them for months in a catalogue,
    so when they came, I drew their sweet leather
        across my cheek. I could have chugged

them like a beer. And then I knelt with a trowel
    to bury them. Barehanded, skinning my knuckles,
        I filled the hole, stomped earth down. The deal

was to hush the monkey of my mind that shrieks
    for more, more. *This far,* I wanted to tell it,
        no further. Why? Because the snakes

I keep, really keep me? Or maybe because I've learned
    the hot blaze of my love for stuff like gloves
        will chill to ashes, leave me vacant

and needing more. The blue coat that dreamed me
    every night into its sleeves hangs in my closet
        unworn. I'm mad to own stuff, okay,

but forever. A gold circle, to keep without end,
    or the green gloves of the oak in summer,
        flashing sunlight, waving in the wind.

Snapshots in a broken camera — that's what I want.
    Look how the sky molds itself to my backyard,
        yet doesn't leave a single fingerprint!

Body Parts

Some of the National Museum of Health and Medicine's
most unsettling stuff is . . . amputated body parts from soldiers
wounded during the Civil War.

NPR Web site

Think how one soldier, on every anniversary
    of his amputation, brought blood-red tulips
to his leg and sat by the glass case,

both hands on one knee,
    his thoughts electrifying the space
between him and what he cannot quite give up —

hanging in that interval, like the shadow
    between a maple and the earth it loves.
I've noticed the way a porch

inclines from its house
    to see how far it can go without permission,
but hoping to hang on for now —

of two minds about wanting to get away.
    It's like coloring outside the lines,
like testing deep water beyond the buoy,

like venturing into outer space,
    daring to edge farther and farther
off the base in schoolyard games.

It's practice, isn't it? A way of thinking
    about the day that the body parts,
the soul flies up to heaven.

Gift

For a hundred miles
   the fields have worn
      beards of ugly stubble
         and night is falling
and you can't find
   a lover, not on AM or FM,
      and the hand at the tollbooth
         wears a glove
so as not to touch you.
   You pay for yourself,
      then for the car behind you,
so someone pushing headlights
   through the heavy dark
      will feel luck
         go off like a Roman candle,
so she'll give a car length
   to the maniac who cuts her off,
and you, there in your lonely bubble,
   can think of each taillight,
      each anonymous fender
         as a friend.

Tracks

Or To Put It Another Way

She is following the voices
as I once followed a car
in darkness, the taillights
like two pieces of red fire
smeared by rain on
my windshield. I didn't know
what I wanted or why,
but I was resolute, a swaying
bundle, steering through wild
curves, mad with the need to catch
someone I thought I recognized.

Or to put it another way,
my mother is becoming my child,
a terrified fawn, standing between
the barbed wire and my car,
its nose sniffing
to catch the scent of home,
its ears alert as two tiny sound dishes
to catch any twitch in
the long, fox-colored weeds.

What I mean is
my mother is leaving us,
has already forgotten us,
concentrating on the voices.
Because it takes concentration
to die properly, to find
the way, to enter
all that terrible glory.

Spirits

March rocks us in its hammock
of purple sky. Snow retreats.
Thunder has not yet cleared its throat
and found a voice. Silence scours
the tin kettle of earth.

At my desk now, I think of my friend
who has vanished from the earth.
All morning I have been reaching for her with
this noun, that verb, but even the most delicate
sentence blunders against her absence
and comes unraveled. What are words, but
vapor? If I could eat with her —
a peach, some bread, a bit of cheese —
I would ask her what she's learned.

Driving at night, you cannot hear
the swell of traffic traveling
in the other direction,
but you can see headlights
scribbling out a journey.
And you wish them well.

Sparrows at Zero

When snow covers the azaleas
with its hoary wisdom,
and our terra-cotta pots
wear white hats of surrender,
and sparrows puff up
dreadfully in the cedar
against the cold, I pull on
my dead father's hunting jacket
and step from the room of language
with its beautiful, treacherous
human motives into silence
cold enough to kill me,
frostbite so quick it whittles all
to a fierce will to live.
Standing here in the frozen chamber
of a sparrow's mind, I can hear
someone in the room of language:
May these sunflower seeds
ignite the sun in them.
May these sparrows be lanterns
that light their own way home.

Little Blessing for My Floater

— *After George Herbert*

This tiny ruin in my eye, small
flaw in the fabric, little speck
of blood in the egg, deep chip
in the windshield, North Star,
polestar, floater that doesn't
float, spot where my hand is not,
little piton nailing every rock
I see, no matter if that image
turns to sand, or sand to sea,
I embrace you, piece of absence
that reminds me what I will be —
all dark some day unless God
rescues me, oh speck
that might still teach me how to see.

Write about Something You Know

The inexactness of sleep, for instance,
how some mornings I swing my feet
to floorboards more unreliable than planks
of light. I pad downstairs, my slippers
trailing from my heels like feathers,
the thread that stitches my bones so loose,
a draft could separate me from them.

I feel the pull of the earth as I lift
breakfast plates and listen for the school bus.
My son's hands hop like toads on the table.
We sit in fellowship with Einstein
and Alexander, who wept when
he had no more worlds to conquer.

As my child climbs on the bus, his kiss,
like the known world, fades on my cheek.
When I walk into the house alone,
I see in the mirror, walking toward me,
myself, middle-aged, shimmering between days
as Alexander must have shimmered
the day he tore his map, the world fluttering
in pieces at his feet, his tears drying
in the first wind of that other world
he would have to conquer soon
without sword or language or companion.

The Secret Life of Shadows

This morning a bumblebee
　　scribbled its shadow across
　　　　sunshine towards our azalea,
which stood radiant as a father,

holding a hundred scarlet blossoms
　　in his arms. How long does a bee live?
　　　　Where will it hide this winter?
Just hatched, how does it know

it should nuzzle in one blossom
　　like a lover? It buzzes sideways, then
　　　　practices, rethinking its approach,
little black-and-yellow saddle shoe

suspended in the air, fat pocket
　　watch, humming like a tiny violin
　　　　with its vocation to reorganize
the universe of azaleas. And then

the helicopter rises swiftly,
　　loaded with bags of sweetness.
　　　　The black-and-yellow knot
seems entirely in love with the earth,

like nothing, nothing a human could
　　ever fashion, except later, driving
　　　　behind a sixteen-wheeler,
I see how its shadow sticks to its side,

like the shadow of the bumblebee,
　　a soul stuck to a body,
　　　　in love, briefly, with the earth,
and I watch it at a stop sign

turn right to exit
　　while its blue-gray shadow,
　　　getting a better idea,
keeps moving silently ahead.

St. Charles Seminary

The Guernsey, chewing thoughtfully, might be
a neighbor looking out her window, watching novices

in orange sweatshirts trudge across the seminary lawn.
One's slung a garbage bag over his shoulder,

the other carries a rake and trowel. Fresh from
dawn Aves, they kneel before the congregation

of brown leaves, as if to memorize the gospel of decay.
They practice the discipline of staying put.

They've broken their thoughts as a trainer breaks wild horses,
with halter and bit of prayer. If their attention wanders,

it is not to the cities where they will be sent
separately this spring, with no women and no money,

one trunk of belongings, each. They glance
toward the Monsignor, whose mind is the vault

they hope holds the map to places they've agreed to love,
who now stands behind them on the balcony,

his gloves draped in one hand like quiet animals.
He scans the dawn sky for clues to solve the riddle

of where they belong. A woolly caterpillar creeps
toward a low branch where it will spin a cocoon,

giving itself freely to what it doesn't understand.
It arches its black back — the holy virgin's eyebrow

lifting to acknowledge the gifts of three wise men.

Praying for Rain in Santa Fe

— For Don Murdoch

This is the end of the world, slow motion, this burning,
    burning till earth is parched, the cypress crisping,
        cactus brown, brown grass, brown horizon.

Through the Cathedral hands of the faithful passes a candle.
    Feel the pull of prayer in the hot dark.
        Tell God nothing can live without water,

water, which is 70 percent of what you're praying with,
    rivers longing through you for more water.
        That's when it comes to you:

In prayer lies prayer's answer. In the calling out,
    the visitation. In the arrow lives the target's eye.
        So water rises from its knees, believing water

will come. When rain starts, a fat drop
    joined by her sisters, the sound of dripping like
        a shy nun sneezing, your heart stops with pleasure

and you pick up the cantaloupe you'll have for dinner
    to shake it. The promise inside: flesh
        the color of sunset, the slosh of a whole ocean.

Foreknowledge

I think he planned it, sort of, from the start,
whether he knew they'd choose the fruit or not.
He scattered hints around the garden — what to do
in case they got themselves kicked out. A shirt
of fur around the lamb. The stream converting
water into syllables. Bamboo pipes.
The caps of mushrooms round as wheels.
Bluebirds composing tunes. He knew nothing
they started later would be new. Except he
didn't factor in the thorns, how they would smart
as Adam — leaving — drove one through his foot.
How clever Romans would invent a crown.
He didn't figure weeds could break his heart.

Bell

— *Good Friday, 2004*

Since time flies one way like an arrow,
the sugar can't be stirred out of your oatmeal,
and no matter how long the murderer sobs
on the median strip — *Sorry!* — she can't reverse
her swerve, cannot rescind her drink

before the crash. Was Jesus heartsick
to find history's not a zipper running both ways?
He who loved eternity — its roominess,
its reversibility — did he have to learn
as he grew up that he never could unsay a thing,

once said? And yet today, like all Good Fridays,
he hangs on the cross again. On altars
he hangs. On necklaces. His death is like an X
that rides the wheel of time, showing up again
in ritual, that miniature eternity, that spring

re-sprung. Dear God, there in your big eternity,
remember that your hands and feet can never
be unscarred again. Hear these words spoken
by a body that suffers, by a tongue
that will stiffen and be gone.

Have mercy on us who love time.
May this prayer be a tire that rolls
over every inch of whatever way
will find you. May it be a bell
which can never be unrung.

Thanks

— *After Gerard Manley Hopkins*

for September sun like a sharp thread
    that strings and pulls me
down the footpath, nearly blind, toward
    the dark woods. For the hawk kiting

on high sheen above the field
    as I cross the footbridge.
For the water's slather, for bittersweet,
    stone flowers, slagmire, silt, sediment

rushing into the slurp of gravity. Thanks even
    for seek and cover, for the seam that
opens in the hay, mouse tail splitting the gold,
    ears sleeked back, frozen against

the plummet, wings folding silent
    as umbrellas, bill hooked, steel
cables grabbing, hauling up. Thanks
    for fierce, fast, for finality,

for let-go, limp, at last. Thanks for not
    covering up what I can't grasp,
and for sunlight, still as strong
    as harp strings, holding earth to heaven.

What the Trees Say

At breakfast, the heart of the egg looks like pure
gold. Sunlight lifts the morning like a lever,
and even before I step outside, I see a river
of sparrows rise and scatter through the dawn.

That's when I tell myself, *Look here,*
you don't have to hurry. Don't have to arrive
anywhere on time. Don't have to decide how far
to walk across the lawn or whether to carry on
into the woods. I pull on my jacket. Breezes scatter
the yellow leaves. The trees are whispering,

It's fall. Got to strip down. Got to let the sky in here,
make a place for birds. Got to reach further
down in earth. Got to hunker, children,
got to hold still enough to feel the wings flutter.

Perspective

In medieval paintings a cobbler would stand inches high
    beside a saint, whose moral stature
filled the canvas. That is, until Brunelleschi thought up

single-point perspective. Lines receding to a speck
    on the horizon. Once people saw, they
dreamt about it — statues and churches kneeling

to the viewer at the commanding point.
    Each of us at the center! The great
myth of the personal. A brigade of art teachers

swung that myth in buckets to the next teachers
    until, generations later, it bears
the heft of Truth. That is, it did. Until the night

I drove the death car, when the sky slit open
    to admit two headlights, double moons
drilling larger and larger holes through darkness

as they bore their terrible gift, two thousand pounds
    of metal, toward me, and suddenly I saw the flaw
in Brunelleschi's myth of the personal. Which of us

can bear to have the world hurled into her lap?
    I swerved then, or something swerved me,
spinning the steel off center so the car missed me.

I picked the lock of the improbable, floated
    back to two-point perspective. I am a tiny patron
suspended in a medieval painting — *that* one, wearing

her everyday red hat and blue cloak,
    keeping her face businesslike,
trying not to say *Aha* as she strides up the golden sky.

Resolutions

I Make My X Here

This morning, while I was driving, a poem came to me,
so pure, so simple, Keats himself could not conceive it,
and then, turning onto Lombard Street, I lost it.

My first novel, five years in the writing, leapt
like an antelope, but it was stolen from our back porch.
To preserve it, I have never written another.

Things are not as good now as they were. But that's no
surprise this mediocre winter Thursday evening
with its ticking radiators and fireplace odors.

The miracle is that I can still remember how once or twice
the sky opened and a thousand feathers rocked down.
I make my X here, to mark where it happened.

Think of how, in the San Francisco earthquake,
William Keith watched his two thousand landscapes
flame orange, then die to rubies, then to ashes.

The next day he started to repaint them
in praise of what he lost. In praise of going on.

Staying Power

— *In appreciation of Maxim Gorky at the*
International Convention of Atheists, 1929

Like Gorky, I sometimes follow my doubts
outside and question the metal sky,
longing to have the fight settled, thinking,
I can't go on like this, and finally I say,

All right, it is improbable — *all right, there*
is *no God.* And then, as if I'm focusing
a magnifying glass on dry leaves, *God* blazes up.
It's the attention, maybe, to what isn't

there that makes the notion flare like
a forest fire until I have to spend the afternoon
spraying it with the hose to put it out. Even
on an ordinary day when a friend calls,

tells me they've found melanoma,
complains that the hospital is cold, I whisper, *God.*
God, I say as my heart turns inside out.
Pick up any language by the scruff of its neck,

wipe its face, set it down on the lawn,
and I bet it will toddle right into the godfire
again, which — though they say it doesn't
exist — can send you straight to the burn unit.

Oh, we have only so many words to think with.
Say God's not fire, say anything, say God's
a phone, maybe. You know you didn't order a phone,
but there it is. It rings. You don't know who it could be.

You don't want to talk, so you pull out
the plug. It rings. You smash it with a hammer

till it bleeds springs and coils and clobbered-up
metal bits. It rings again. You pick it up

and a voice you love whispers hello.

The Stars of Last Resort

Imagine someday the splurge
    drains out of fall.
        Holding a melon,
            you know a creek of light
streams inside its rough burlap ball,
    but if you cut it open,
        you know stars will fall,
            extinguished in the dark.
You know the quarrel
    of the squeaky porch swing,
        know the cold that stacks goldfish like knives
            will kill them before the winter's over.
And you can't not think
    about your friend, who leapt
        from the Ferris wheel
            of months too soon,
before it came full circle.
    Suppose your sixty summers
        dull the summer sun,
blow fuzz across the lens.
    Maybe night comes sooner
        and more chill,
            but it still brings luminaries
as if gathered for a cause.
    They bend, surprisingly,
        the generous stars,
            laying their hands together
        in applause.

Pardon

She stands, palms up, alone, a woman
who should not be alone, mother, watching
as I get in my car, driving to make dinner
for my child and husband in another city,
my heart cantering like a stallion

alone down the hard road of guilt.
Later, as I water plants, stash groceries,
I almost hear her — *What am I to you now but*
a root pulled up? A car to junk when you've
driven its heart out? — my mind spinning

in the muddy track of fault it cannot exit
till it has permission from her, my
mother, the woman I ricocheted from
when I was twenty, to root my life
in a distant city, loving the distance,

not seeing that it was permanent, not seeing
that my own children would leave me
to take root in distant cities. And then
the phone rings. She's calling to report
the sun is doing a striptease on the horizon.

She's amazed by the tiny wrecker-truck
of a praying mantis. By news that her eighty-year-old
friend is getting married. By her capacity
to be surprised. She goes on and on,
talking, this Matriarch of Amazements.

Connections

After, against, among, around. How I admire
prepositions, small as they are, nothing
but safety pins, their lives given to
connecting. They are paid help,
maids in black uniforms who pass
hors d'oeuvres. Or better, they're the joy
that leaps between us when we get to
know them. Without connection, what
can survive? Because the lawn
waits for the sun to wake it from
its winter nap, we say sunlight
lies *on* the grass. Even the simplest jar
connects — jar under moonlight, on
counter, jar in water. It was prepositions
in the Valley of Dry Bones that stitched
the femur to the heel, the heel to the foot bone.
And afterwards, they got up to dance.
Between, beside, within may yet keep
the chins and breasts from tumbling off
Picasso's women. If I could, I would
make prepositions the stars of grammar,
like the star which traveled the cobalt sky
that night sweet Jesus lay in his cradle,
pulling the wise and devious kings
toward Bethlehem, and us behind them,
trekking from the rim of history toward him.

Plenty

Sunlight is breaking into colors around me
    like a catastrophe I can neither
        shake nor explain —
how the sun's gold finger
    dusts the tops of maples.
        How the maple's articulate roots
wrestle with dumb earth.
        How our houses, breaking free of foliage,
            stare candidly at one another's naked bodies.
Time washes all the bridges out, dismembers
    the maples, expires like a parking meter.
        We check and recheck our watches and
pay costly tickets anyway.
        Yet look how small a thing can defeat time.
        I made this from bits of salvage —
my own breath
    and a few secondhand words.

Helping the Morning

After the graveside, after the ride home, after
   a winter of drought, the chain
      and padlock on my heart,

morning shows up at my bedside,
   almost too late, like a big sister
      holding a glass of water,

and I drink, glancing through the window
   at the tiny red barn flung
      into the lap of the brown valley below.

I am amazed at the silent, terrible wonder
   of my health. I am giddy at the lack of war.
      I want to help the morning.

I pray the bedpost, the windowpanes.
   I put our children on two doorknobs,
      Our sick friends in mirrors.

Like the aperture of a camera, the morning opens
   and keeps opening until the room is filled
      with rosy light and I could believe

anything: that grass might turn green again,
   that clouds the size of my hand
      might swell, might drift in, bringing rain.

Art

Signs of use, of age, of damage are esteemed as part of the life of Japanese scrolls.

Program, Koetsu Exhibition,
Philadelphia Museum of Art

On this scroll I see new tracks
crossing winter fields, cold rain,
river cutting through plains,
night falling. Let me not ask for
untrampled snow. May I love
the moon, no longer full,
but worn to a slice. Bless fragments,
corners, crumbs, and spare parts.
Let them remind me of what
they were, unbroken. May I
stop listening for the wild steps
of morning, which will not scrape
my sill again. I will praise in the rain
what remains of the afternoon.

Centering

Remember, the frightened sparrow's
flapping finally calmed into a pattern
just before it found the window and
escaped. I mean, while we squinted
and pointed in the dairy aisle,
that trapped mind *did* circle, after all,
in louvered sunlight. Think of
the housewife's rag circling a windowpane
one lazy morning, or a painter's thumb,
smudging his purple sunrise with
little blushing clouds. It's the return
I'm talking about. Getting to do it over.
Black cat circling her cushion,
antediluvian duo whisking
the ballroom floor like brooms,
or lips looping *oh, oh, oh*, mouth
in love with the sound. Oh, after
a while it feels inevitable,
the long blue pull of the mind
that keeps finding more in less
until the will bends and circles
home to stillness that feels final, true.

The Dogs That Do Not Bite

— For Molly

Red Rover. Attila the Hun. Lassie 1, 2, and 3,
and a queue of The Abandoned — dachshund
with slipped disk, white Pekinese with plum eyes,
pit bull quivering in a Nebraska snowstorm
with jaws strong enough to break our arms,
those cynical hobos who auditioned, working us
with sweet, treble songs. Their hearts heartworm-
infested, their tails pinwheeling. In those days,
I hadn't studied Hegel or hoisted cabernet at sunset.
I had no standards. As long as they loved us,
as long as my mother would buy them food,
I wanted all the ones that didn't bite us.
They were dangerous as weather systems,
the winds that rose and threatened overnight
but still haven't sacked our coastline, the hurricanes
that haven't sunk their teeth in. What is this
odd eagerness to please that moves through
the Spirit on the face of the deep? Who can say
all the names of the dogs that do not bite?

Ownership

— *For Jack Leax*

Sitting by the window, she watches
   a chipping-sparrow nag a seed from the feeder.
Her hand wants to touch its feathers, feel it flicker,

starting brown trouble in the old routine of green.
   When it flies away, how easily it carries
the sky on its back. She'd love to give it to her husband.

This is for us, she would write on the card,
   and hang its cage in the kitchen. Lately her body,
she notices, wants to own everything,

to be everywhere at once. But even a window
   has an inside and an outside.
Her body always here, the sparrow always there,

wearing its own brown shirt,
   little machine for joy, what she can never
count on, what's present every morning.

Looking for Ruby Earrings on Portobello Road

Not to want it *all* is a sort of defect —
the porcelain cows, socks made from flags,
scarves fluttering against the blue throat of the sky,
hotdogs, broaches made of forks, paper cockatoos,
an organ grinder with three blind cats,
a lover wrapped around a saxophone.
Listen as he coaxes it to love him.

The perfect earring, if I could find it, will tumble
through a sidewalk grate soon enough,
and yet I drift across the street, waiting
to be gulled, trying to catch fire again.
Then the notes of the full-throated sax
rise, and my eyes rise with them
to stones gleaming on black velvet
in a stall cluttered with celestial junk

and I laugh as the saxophone is laughing,
because the stone is the least of it —
cheap glass or plastic — just an instrument
to play on. And the holy river of desire
runs wide. I buy the earrings,
which call me to the world we can never keep
but must, nevertheless, adore,
it being all we know of eternity.

Fleeting

A fur-splendid, fierce-eyed collie trots by,
her black lips stretched into a smile, head up,
panting, to join her man, who has whistled
Come! in the amphitheatre of oaks
at the end of Baird and Walnut, cavernous enough
for herds of moose to pass.

Last night's rain darkens the tree bark.
Now sunlight descends around his blue jacket
like harp strings, touching his shoulders,
breaking to arpeggios. Radiance
in sheets, so beautiful it's catastrophic,
rubbing away what seems most plainly Earth.

The trees, the man, the collie tremble
and collapse to light. Such brilliance
that I have to look down to earth
where toadstools have tossed up cheap seats
to watch beside the crabgrass.

All Told

With machines and tubes
we tried to postpone it
as long as possible,
leaving Him to idle
in his black limo
in your driveway, stubbing
out his cigarette
as you slipped out the back door,
swam across the pond
beneath the water,
shook yourself dry,
and hitched for
a distant suburb.
He picked up
his cell and tried
and tried to call you

who kept gathering
light as you sped
toward radiance,
shedding our dark
sorrow behind you,
showing us ways to
do it, and now, here we are,
years later, standing together
in the cooling fires
of our own deaths,
saying *All told,* as we
recount our stories,
practiced now, knowledge
rinsing through us
easily as hot water
through tea leaves.

Leaving the Planetarium

— For Jack

"Old things are passed away. Behold, everything is become new."

2 Corinthians 5:17

You pull at my sweater, weeping,
and I lift you from your seat.
We stumble out together. It's too much
for a five-year-old, too much red
fire raining down. Years from now,
long after your great-great-grandchildren are dead,
the sun, having burned its own body up,
will reach out like a jealous father
to eat his children — Mercury first, then Venus.
The next day there will be a last
perfect sunrise, and afterwards
an arm of fire will embrace
the one Earth
you think you cannot do without.
But I tell you,
my tiny flash of light,
you will be blazing like a sun by then,
and everyone you care for
will have swum into sharper focus,
like a picture that's developed slowly.
By then we will remember the Earth
only as the place where, long ago,
we first learned how to love.

Holding Action

Letters, be the memory of this moment,
Ruth's three-legged Golden Lab
sniffing for news beneath the hedge,
grass glittering with rain,
the bird feeder mangled by our car.

Years from now I want to remember
how we walked the splendid earth
and saw it. When children read this
and smile at its old-fashioned vision,
then words, stubborn little boxcars

lugging meaning across the rickety
wood bridge to the future, hold,
hold. Couple against time, bear
the red geranium, the slender birch —
you, sentences — glitter against

the massive dark of nothing. Tell
of feet that buffed this doorsill
till it gleams, of cartwheeling
children. Remember the Rosetta
stone, the hum of Xerox machines,

remember monks copying, how
a prisoner in solitary picked up
a pebble to scribble stories
on the wall. Letters, I tell you,
even if your paper yellows in the attic,

even if it's torn and thrown into the sea,
each of you separate from your brothers,
swim through the ocean, row across
the sky, walk through the wasteland,
find a reader. Stay together. Hold.